THE
BIG
TIME

ADRIAN PETERSON

AARON FRISCH

CREATIVE  EDUCATION

ADRIAN PETERSON

TABLE OF CONTENTS

MEET ADRIAN

Adrian gets the ball. He charges forward and knocks a defender over. The crowd roars. But Adrian is not done yet. He spins, then he runs all the way to the end zone. Touchdown!

In football, some running backs are very fast. Others are very powerful. Minnesota Vikings star Adrian Peterson is both! And he never seems to get tired. That is why he is nicknamed "All-Day."

....

Adrian might catch passes or run other players over

ADRIAN'S CHILDHOOD

Adrian was born March 21, 1985, in Palestine, Texas. His parents had both been good athletes. As a boy, Adrian had a lot of energy. He and his older brother Brian always ran around.

As a little kid and a teenager, Adrian was always fast

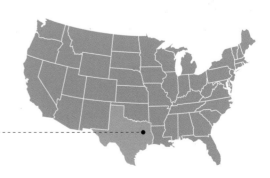

PALESTINE, TEXAS

GETTING INTO FOOTBALL

Brian died after being hit by a car when Adrian was seven. When Adrian was 13, his dad went to jail for selling drugs. Playing football helped Adrian deal with these hard times.

....

Adrian with his dad, Nelson, in 2009

Adrian was very fast. He became a football and *track and field* star in high school. In his last game, Adrian *rushed* for six touchdowns. Then he went to the University of Oklahoma to play football.

The University of Oklahoma Sooners are one of the top college football teams

THE BIG TIME

Adrian played college football for three seasons. Then he went into the National Football League (NFL). The Vikings *drafted* Adrian in 2007. In his 8th game, he ran for 296 yards. That set a new NFL *record*!

....

Adrian was the seventh player drafted in 2007

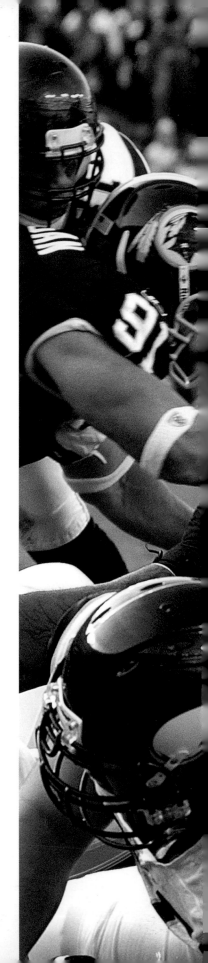

In 2008, Adrian rushed for 1,760 yards. That was the most in the NFL. In 2009, he helped the Vikings win 13 games and almost get to the Super Bowl. Most people thought he was the best running back in football.

Through the 2011 season, Adrian scored 64 touchdowns as an NFL player

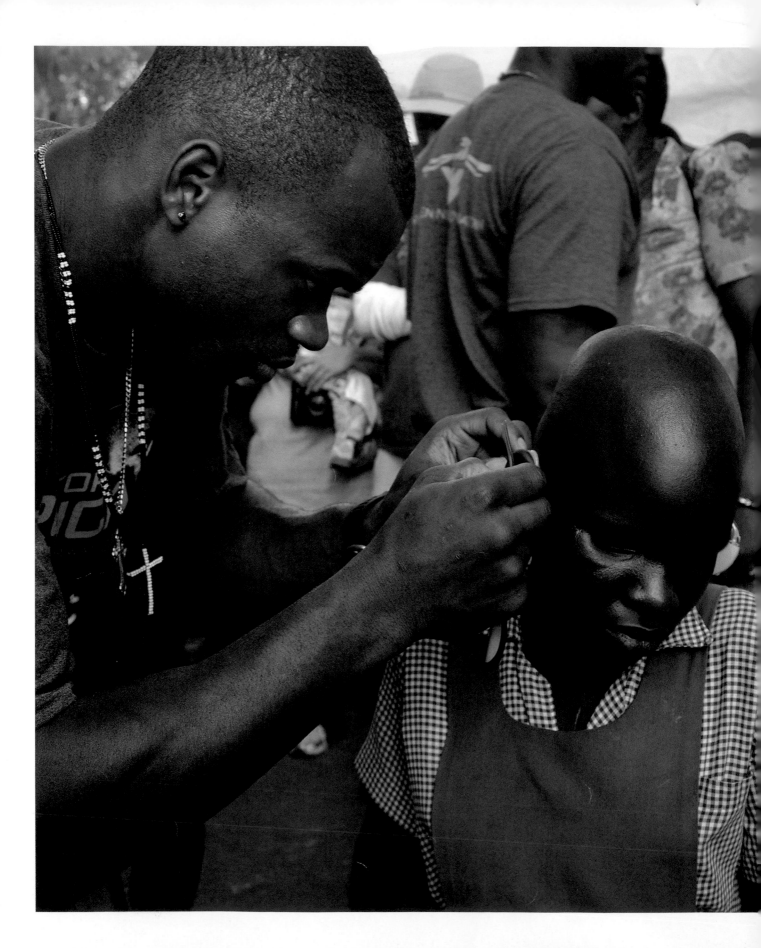

OFF THE FIELD

When he is not playing football, Adrian spends time with his two kids. He likes to play poker and listen to rap music, too. Adrian gives away food to hungry people and helps teach kids about the game of football.

....

Adrian helping a girl in Africa use a hearing aid

WHAT IS NEXT?

In 2011, Adrian was having another big season. But then he hurt his left knee. Adrian believed he would be back and better than ever after having **surgery**. He hoped to play in the Super Bowl soon!

··

Adrian was 27 when the 2012 NFL season started

WHAT ADRIAN SAYS ABOUT …

HIS FAMILY

"When I go out on the field, I just put it in my mind that I'm playing for my family."

HIS GOAL

"I want to win four or five championship rings. That's how I dream. I dream big."

THE WAY HE RUNS

"I run angry. Football allows me to take out some of my pain on the field."

GLOSSARY

drafted picked to be on a team; in a sports draft, teams take turns choosing players

record something that is the most or the best ever

rushed ran with the football

surgery when doctors fix a body part that is sick or injured

track and field a sport that includes races on a round track and jumping and throwing contests

READ MORE

Gitlin, Marty. *Adrian Peterson: Record-Setting Running Back*. Minneapolis: Abdo, 2012.

Sandler, Michael. *Adrian Peterson*. New York: Bearport, 2010.

WEB SITES

Minnesota Vikings Kids Club
http://www.vikings.com/fans/kids-club/index.html
This is the Web site of Adrian's team, the Minnesota Vikings.

Pro Football Reference
http://www.pro-football-reference.com/players/P/PeteAd01.htm
This page lists Adrian's statistics and all the honors he has won.

INDEX

PUBLISHED BY Creative Education
P.O. Box 227, Mankato, Minnesota 56002
Creative Education is an imprint of The Creative Company
www.thecreativecompany.us

DESIGN AND PRODUCTION BY Christine Vanderbeek
ART DIRECTION BY Rita Marshall
PRINTED IN the United States of America

PHOTOGRAPHS BY AP (Ronen Zilberman), Dreamstime (Scott Anderson), Getty Images (Tom Dahlin, Tom Hauck, Paul Jasienski, Laizure Photo/WireImage, Joe Robbins, Richard Schultz/NFLPhotoLibrary, Harry E. Walker/MCT), iStockphoto (Anthia Cumming, Pingebat), Newscom (Image of Sport Image of Sport Photos, Steve Terill/AFP)

LIBRARY OF CONGRESS CATALOGING-IN-PUBLICATION DATA
Frisch, Aaron.
Adrian Peterson / Aaron Frisch.
p. cm. — (The big time)
Includes bibliographical references and index.
Summary: An elementary introduction to the life, work, and popularity of Adrian Peterson, a professional football star who became the all-time leading rusher for the Minnesota Vikings.

ISBN 978-1-60818-335-7
1. Peterson, Adrian—Juvenile literature. 2. Football players—United States—Biography—Juvenile literature. 3. Running backs (Football)—United States—Biography—Juvenile literature. I. Title.
GV939.P477F75 2013
796.332092—dc23 [B]   2012013475

First edition
9 8 7 6 5 4 3 2 1